DRUGS
THE COMPLETE STORY

TOBACCO

Philip Cohen

STECK-VAUGHN
L I B R A R Y
A Division of Steck-Vaughn Company

Austin, Texas

CONTENTS

> *The huge tobacco companies . . . spend billions urging people . . . to buy products that have been proved to be harmful to health.*

> *In the developing countries the tobacco companies can now make their biggest profits.*

> *The loss of food . . . could be the difference between life and death in countries where children often do not survive beyond five.*

CONTENTS

GLOSSARY

addiction: the forming of a dependence on a drug.
BAT: British-American Tobacco Industries.
bronchitis: the inability to clear the lungs and air passages of phlegm, leading to infection and breathlessness.
Buerger's Disease: an illness that only affects smokers and which can result in limbs having to be amputated.
carbon monoxide: a poisonous gas contained in cigarette smoke which hinders the release of oxygen into the body.
cholesterol: a fatty substance that occurs in the brain and blood cells which can be harmful if there is too much of it.
curing: the process of drying tobacco leaves to preserve the color and flavor.
diversify: to channel the operations of a company into more than one type of product or activity so that the company is not wholly dependent on a single product or activity.
emphysema: a disease that breaks down the walls of the air sacs throughout the lungs and makes it difficult to breathe.
hemoglobin: the oxygen-carrying protein in red blood cells.
instructors: the representatives of the tobacco industry who give help and advice on growing tobacco to the farmers.
nicotine: a poisonous substance found in the tobacco plant.
passive smoking: the inhalation of smoke from cigarettes smoked by other people.
sponsorship: a gift of financial support from a company to an event, to link that event with the name of the company.
subsidiary: a smaller company that is all or partly owned or run by a larger parent company.
Surgeon General: the chief American medical officer for health.
tobacco tar: a dark, sticky substance that is the result of the burning of a cigarette.

THE ARGUMENT
ABOUT TOBACCO

Smoking is big news. It is a major economic, political, and social, as well as a health issue of our time. Nobody can ignore the consequences of it, which are both personal and social. It is important, for example, for us to consider our own personal health and how much smoking interferes with it. Critics of tobacco condemn smoking because they think that cigarette smoke affects everyone who breathes it in, not just the smoker.

> *... the huge tobacco companies ... spend billions urging people all over the world to buy products that have been proved to be harmful to health.*

Smokers, on the other hand, may argue that everyone has a right to choose whether to smoke or not, and that their smoking affects only them. The social effects of the power and wealth of the huge tobacco companies cannot be ignored either. These companies spend billions urging people all over the world to buy products that have been proved to be harmful to health. The tobacco companies argue that they are only supplying the market for cigarettes that already exists. No wonder the smoking issue causes such argument.

The propaganda war

One of the Surgeon General's warnings on cigarette packages reads "quitting smoking now greatly reduces serious risks to your health." One of the warnings inserted in magazine ads declares "smoking causes lung cancer, heart disease,

Margaret Thatcher, a former British Prime Minister, launched Europe Against Cancer 1989, aimed at promoting cancer information.

emphysema, and may complicate pregnancy." The words "addiction" and "death" go unmentioned due to strong tobacco industry protests.

A government warning is very important in reducing deaths and illness from smoking. However, every year governments receive millions in revenue in the form of taxes on tobacco products. No governments have yet felt able to turn their backs on that kind of income or to face the constitutional issues restricting a person's right to smoke. Nor do politicians want to come into conflict with the tobacco companies, who have a lot of influence and argue that they provide jobs worldwide.

> . . .*every year governments receive millions in revenue in the form of taxes on tobacco products. No governments have yet felt able to turn their backs on that kind of income or face other constitutional issues.*

In the media, there is a constant war of words waged between the representatives of the tobacco industry and health campaigners. For instance, in the United States, it is estimated that the number of people who die from smoking-related illnesses is 6,700 per week. One newspaper recently carried a report on a new smokeless cigarette, which is likely to be thought of as a significant development by people who are in danger of passive smoking by inhaling other people's smoke. However, a representative of the tobacco industry wrote in, attacking the observation that "secondary smoke damages everybody's health," and claiming that the media had the whole issue out of proportion. Evidence has now been collected that passive smoking is indeed harmful.

The voice of the United States' tobacco industry, the Tobacco Institute, claims that the war against cancer is considered by people to be a war against smokers. "No one really knows whether this personalized warfare against millions of Americans will prevent a single case of lung cancer or heart disease." Opponents of the industry call this view "the big lie."

Throughout the developing world people are being encouraged to smoke, even in remote Papua New Guinea where this Simbai dancer lives.

TOBACCO

The Surgeon General expressed his anger when laws were changed which meant that the government no longer had to put warnings about addiction on cigarette packs. He condemned the attitude of people who will not recognize the dangers of smoking and stressed that a smoker is "an addict of the most addictive drug we have in our society."

> . . . a smoker is "an addict of the most addictive drug we have in our society."

Employers and employees

The worldwide nature of the tobacco industry means that it controls thousands of people, whether they are small farmers in the developing countries, those who work in its factories processing the tobacco, or the people at the end of the chain — the smokers. It is a global industry with enormous influence. Yet tobacco companies are aware that the tide of public opinion in the developed world has been gradually moving against them. As a result, they have moved much of their production to the developing countries and begun to promote other kinds of products and services.

The people who run the tobacco plantations can make a living out of tobacco, but they are often dependent on the tobacco companies for this living. This is because they often borrow money from tobacco companies to set up their farms and have to repay these loans. Also, the governments of these countries may become overdependent on the money that can be earned from tobacco exports. This can lead to the situation where a country that is producing tobacco may not even be growing enough food to support its population. Whether farmers should be growing cash crops like tobacco or food crops is a crucial issue.

There is also environmental damage caused by the felling of millions of trees for the wood that is used in curing or treating the tobacco before it can be processed into cigarettes. It is already known that the removal of the forests changes the pattern of weather in the areas where the trees formerly grew. This in turn leads to erosion of soil, and desert conditions or flooding, depending on the amount of rainfall in the area.

THE ARGUMENT ABOUT TOBACCO

Once tobacco has been grown, harvested, and processed, the resulting products such as cigarettes and cigars have to be sold. Advertising plays an essential role in this, particularly as it has to make products seem appealing when they are known to be bad for health.

The tobacco industry goes to great lengths to promote its products. It uses attractive images of youth, success, and wealth. It also sponsors many forms of sports in order to fix the name of a particular brand in the mind of the public. However, the advertising of tobacco is banned from radio and television.

> *"You don't want cigarettes. You don't need them. Look what they've done to me. Do you want to end up like this?"*

It is clear that many smokers want to quit, and some have tried to do so, with varying degrees of success. Many succeed, which is why consumption of cigarettes is at its lowest point in about forty years. It is obviously up to the individual and much can be learned from seeing how smoking affects others. One person described how, on a city bus, he saw two young teenage boys trying to beg a cigarette from an elderly man who was coughing badly. They taunted him when he refused, and the man eventually turned on them, saying, "You don't want cigarettes. You don't need them. Look what they've done to me. Do you want to end up like this?"

THE TOBACCO MARKET

Tobacco is grown, and then smoked in the form of cigarettes, cigars, and pipe tobacco, all over the world. For many years the market for tobacco products has been supplied mainly by farmers in North America who have a long tradition of growing tobacco going back to the eighteenth century. However, these farmers have faced increasing competition from small peasant farmers in China, Africa, India, and Brazil who see tobacco as a way of achieving a reasonable income in a short time.

> *. . . small peasant farmers in China, Africa, India, and Brazil . . . see tobacco as a way of achieving a reasonable income in a short time.*

The producers

China is by far the largest tobacco producer in the world — a fact that might surprise many people. In 1988 China produced two million tons of leaf tobacco compared to the world's second largest producer, the U.S., with 592,000 tons. However, in world terms this is not significant because the Chinese export very little and consume most of the crop themselves. There are 200 million smokers in China, which has over 1,000 different brands of cigarettes, none of which is known outside that vast country.

Chinese cigarettes used to be handmade locally. After the Maoist revolution in the 1950s, production continued on a local commune basis, and each commune was encouraged to be self-sufficient. In recent years, production has become much

China is the world's largest tobacco producer and manufactures cigars and over 1,000 different brands of cigarettes. These brands used to be made locally but are now produced in 83 factories.

more centralized, with 83 factories employing 90,000 workers. One factory alone in Shanghai turns out 41 billion cigarettes a year. With a total population of more than a billion, China is very attractive to foreign companies because of the cheap labor they can employ there.

> *There are 200 million smokers in China, which has over 1,000 different brands of cigarettes, none of which is known outside that vast country.*

Since 1980, three Western tobacco companies have been allowed to produce cigarettes in China for tourists and foreigners. However, the Chinese are not allowed to buy these particular brands. Unless some control is kept on the production and import of cigarettes, health problems for the people of China could dramatically increase.

In the U.S., where 50 million Americans smoke a total of over 600 billion cigarettes a year, the tobacco is produced by

TOBACCO

This is the Duke homestead in North Carolina. The Dukes were one of the key families in developing the tobacco industry in the U.S. after the Civil War. Profits were later given to set up universities and hospitals.

600,000 farmers mainly in the southern states of North and South Carolina, Kentucky, Virginia, Tennessee, Georgia, Florida, and Alabama. Many of the farming families have been growing tobacco for 200 years, but the process has become more modernized. Instead of burning wood to create the heat that will dry the tobacco leaves, liquid gas and gasoline are used. Combine harvesters are usually used now, whereas formerly the crop was handpicked. As with other agricultural products the federal government gives money to the farmers through loans which helps to keep the price of tobacco high and, in turn, provides the government with tax revenues.

Brazil is the third biggest producer of tobacco, having greatly increased the size of its industry in the 1960s. In the southern part of the country around the city of Santa Cruz at least 100,000 small farmers grow tobacco and boast that Brazil is the "tobacco capital of the world," a claim that is strongly contested in the southern U.S. One Brazilian farmer said, "We need people to smoke more so we can make more money."

After Brazil come other producers as far apart as India, the Soviet Union, and several other Eastern European countries, followed by Turkey, Greece, and Zimbabwe. Countries like Brazil and Zimbabwe export some of their tobacco in exchange for foreign currency. Despite the fact that the U.S. grows tobacco, it still imports large amounts from Brazil and Turkey because tobacco is produced more cheaply there than the home-grown variety. This is because wages paid to workers in developing countries are often very low.

> *"We need people to smoke more so we can make more money."*

The tobacco companies

In recent years, governments have increased taxes on cigarettes. That, together with higher prices and greater public awareness of the health hazards of smoking, has caused sales of cigarettes to drop worldwide.

Many of the farmers around the world are under contract to one of the huge multinational tobacco companies that control the industry. As fears about the health risks from smoking have risen in the West, the giant companies have taken two steps. First, they set up smaller subsidiary companies to produce tobacco and cigarettes in developing countries where it was cheaper to employ people and there was a growing market for cigarettes. Most people there were not aware of the harmful effects of tobacco.

Then, the companies diversified into other products. That is, instead of just producing tobacco and selling it around the world, they started selling other products and services, like insurance, paper, and cosmetics. R.J. Reynolds Industries which manufactures Camel cigarettes also owns oil refineries and currently owns the Nabisco Company. Multinational tobacco companies also own beer, soft drink, property development, and packaging companies. This diversification means that the tobacco companies are not totally dependent on tobacco if more people stop smoking and the tobacco trade slumps.

TOBACCO

The giant companies of the tobacco industry have begun to diversify into other products. These instant meals are made by Golden Wonder, originally potato chip manufacturers and now owned by Imperial Tobacco in Great Britain.

BAT

British-American Tobacco Industries (BAT) is the biggest tobacco company in the world, employing 300,000 people in 90 countries around the world and having an annual turnover, or amount of business, of well over $30 billion a year. Most of BAT's markets are in developing countries where it expanded early this century, but it also shares in the running of subsidiary companies in the U.S.

Recently, BAT has been trying to move away from producing just tobacco. Its production of tobacco fell from 51 percent of its activity in 1983 to 40 percent in 1987. The interest the company holds in insurance, however, moved from nothing to 22 percent of the total in the same period. BAT now owns discount stores, large insurance groups, and upscale department stores such as Saks Fifth Avenue and Marshall Fields.

BAT dominates the international tobacco industry, normally operating through subsidiary companies in countries such as

Brazil, Germany, Kenya, and South Africa. BAT argues that it is aware of the needs of developing countries and helps them to provide jobs and foreign exchange for their economies.

> *It is in the developing countries that the tobacco companies can now make their biggest profits, but it is there too that they face the biggest questions about their activities.*

There are, however, critics of companies like BAT who argue that it does not control the advertising and promotion of its products in the developing countries in the way it should. They say the farmers in these countries become dependent on the assistance of BAT and are trapped by it. It is in the developing countries that the tobacco companies can now make their biggest profits, but it is there also that they face the biggest questions about their activities.

3

WHO PAYS THE PRICE?

In the 1960s, developing countries contributed about 17 percent of world tobacco production. By 1976, it had reached about 40 percent and it is still increasing. The developing world has offered a rich source of income for the tobacco companies as the market in the developed world has begun to shrink. However, tobacco produced in developing countries, such as those in Africa, is mostly consumed locally, and in some countries, particularly in Asia, there has been an increase in the amount of tobacco consumed.

> *"In times of drought and scarcity of food, the farmer may consider that cultivating a cash crop such as tobacco is a luxury he cannot afford."*

The developed countries had an estimated tobacco growth rate of just over one percent between 1980 and 1985 compared to nearly four percent for the developing world in the same period. Brazil earns a massive $300 million worth of exports from tobacco, which amounts to nearly one billion dollars' worth of tax revenue for the government. The industry provides thousands of jobs in factories processing the tobacco leaf, many to women who earn low wages in bad working conditions.

Most of the farmers in Brazil and other developing countries cultivate small areas and grow tobacco to earn the money needed to support their families. For farmers, tobacco requires a lot of investment, which means that they have to take on large loans from the tobacco companies to finance their operations.

Tobacco plants can be planted with as many as 75,000 plants to the acre. The large leaves must be harvested in dry conditions.

The peasant farmer has to grow both subsistence crops such as corn to feed his family and cash crops like tobacco to earn the income needed to finance the next crop. "In times of drought and scarcity of food the farmer may consider that cultivating a cash crop such as tobacco is a luxury he cannot afford. At the best of times he may only be able to devote a small section of his land to tobacco."

Planting and harvesting

To cultivate tobacco, the earth must first be cleaned to kill the insects and diseases that would spell disaster for the farmer. This is done either with chemicals or by burning the ground. The small tobacco seedlings are sown in carefully tended nurseries where they grow to a height of about four inches (10 cm.). Then they are transplanted to the growing field which has been specially prepared.

There are several different kinds of tobacco, which need different soils to grow in. For example, some tobaccos flourish in light and well-drained soil, while others do well on poor, stony soil. It is important for transplanting that there has been rainfall and that the temperature is warm. During the growing period, the temperature may rise, but the plants have to be watered if there is no further rain.

Tobacco plants can be planted close to one another and there may be as many as 75,000 plants on one acre alone. The plants have to be checked constantly for signs of disease, such as blue mold. After weeding and treating the tobacco plants with fertilizers for about 10 weeks, the crop must be harvested in dry conditions. This is still done mainly by hand to avoid damage to the plant, and the harvest provides jobs for many seasonal workers.

Curing

The tobacco then has to be cured. This term is also used for preserving meat and fruit, but in the case of tobacco, it means drying the leaf so that it can be stored for long periods. Although the process dries the tobacco leaf, it must never be allowed to dry out. It is important that the processed tobacco retains some moisture, and the curing process is a difficult one, requiring several days of careful temperature control and constant tending. The curing process allows the leaves to develop the different tastes and colors that are a feature of tobacco.

> *It is important that processed tobacco should retain some moisture, and the curing process is a difficult one, requiring several days of careful temperature control and constant tending.*

The curing is done in barns. The leaves are hung inside and in the most common process, called flue-curing, warm currents of air are sent in through flues or air vents in the barn walls by means of a furnace outside. On modernized farms, curing is done in bulk and electric fans control the circulation of air.

The process leads to the production of different kinds of leaves. Some are flue-cured, which accounts for 40 percent of world production and produces Virginia tobacco. Curing can also be done using natural air or hanging leaves in the sun for up to three weeks.

Curing, or preserving, tobacco leaves is done in barns. This allows the air to circulate freely between the leaves.

Tobacco leaves are sometimes steamed during curing to prevent them from drying out too much.

TOBACCO

This tobacco auction is at Harare, the capital of Zimbabwe. It is the largest trading area in the world. The tobacco is auctioned rapidly as only 5 seconds are allowed for each bale to be assessed and sold.

The tobacco is then packed and sold. In developing countries, buyers purchase a farmer's entire crop before it is harvested, but in other places such as the U.S., Europe, and Zimbabwe a tobacco auction is held. The leaves are sold very quickly at these auctions. The tobacco is then taken to factories in the same country for manufacture into cigarettes, cigars, or pipe tobacco, or it is taken direct to the ports for shipping overseas.

The farmers and the tobacco companies

In the southern area of Brazil, the farmers have developed the production of Virginia leaf tobacco, which has become very popular on the world market. In the Santa Cruz area, there are regular jobs for some 3,500 people in factories and at the peak of the season about 10,000 people are employed. A subsidiary of BAT called Souza Cruz has controlled the market in Brazil for a long time and is the main supplier of loans for equipment to the small farmer.

WHO PAYS THE PRICE?

The tobacco companies employ people called instructors who visit the farms and advise on where the tobacco is to be planted, the growing process, fertilizers, pesticides, and harvesting. The instructors give out seeds, tools, and other equipment. However, eventually all this has to be paid for by the farmer and will come out of the sale of his produce.

The companies prefer not to run tobacco farms themselves because of the huge investment that would be needed, so they cooperate with the small farmers instead. It is the companies that are the key sources of loans for the farmers and the main source of advice about cultivation and production. It is company buyers who go to the farms and buy up the crops after selecting the best leaves.

In many developing countries, buyers agree to purchase a farmer's whole crop at a fixed price even before it is planted. This gives an advantage to the farmer in that he has a guaranteed sale. The disadvantage is that if he has already agreed on a price and then has a bumper crop of excellent leaf, he cannot haggle for a better price with other buyers. It is in ways like this that the large tobacco companies keep a grip on the market.

An analysis of tobacco growing in five developing countries shows that it can produce a quick, short-term return for small farmers. However, it depends on the ability to borrow money from the government or a big tobacco company. It also depends on whether or not the farmer is able to grow food for his family as well. The tobacco farmer is highly vulnerable in many ways. Besides the financial price, there are other prices that people in developing countries have to pay.

The cost to the environment

So much wood is needed to dry the tobacco leaves that vast areas of the developing world have been stripped bare of trees. In one area of Brazil, the farmers are estimated to use up to 60 million trees in a single year. Researchers estimate that worldwide, the equivalent of three million acres of open forest is stripped of wood for curing every year.

Replanting programs are vital if permanent ecological damage is to be avoided. There is a growing awareness of the danger, and tobacco companies have begun to encourage farmers to devote some of their land to fast-growing trees, and to find alternative sources of fuel. However, the soil is usually not very good for replanting, and it means that there is less land for growing tobacco or food. "Farmers are naturally reluctant to tie up their land for ten years or more to provide fuel which, even now, is still obtainable from outside the farm." Wood remains the most desirable fuel for the farmer although in several countries more coal, gas, and oil are now used.

> "There can be no argument that trees in the tobacco-producing areas are being felled willy nilly and that in the not too distant future there won't be any left at all."

A small farmer in Kenya says, "I have lived here all my life and this area used to be thick with trees. Now after another five years of tobacco, there won't be any trees left." A former employee of BAT (Kenya) has stated, "There can be no argument that trees in the tobacco-producing areas are being felled willy nilly and that in the not too distant future there won't be any left at all."

The effects on the ecology of developing countries is devastating. Tobacco cultivation leaves behind it land that is not fit for food production. In addition to the damage done to the trees, tobacco removes nutrients from the soil at a much faster rate than other crops. Water tables under the soil are badly affected and wells dry up. Tobacco thrives on semiarid land. The result of tobacco production is that the land has less protection against the "march of the desert."

A dangerous habit

The tobacco industry argues that a farmer can just as well grow rice at the same time as growing tobacco. However, the pressure is on to devote more time and land to tobacco in order to make a quick profit.

One study showed that because tobacco companies advertise so heavily in developing countries, poor people may be persuaded to start smoking, spending some of what little cash they have on cigarettes rather than on food. The loss of food and therefore nutrition to the children could be the difference between life and death in countries where children often do not survive beyond the age of five.

Smokers in developing countries also face a risk to their own health as well as to the health of their children. Cigarette consumption has risen massively in developing countries; it is estimated that two-thirds of all new cases of lung cancer are found in these areas. In Pakistan, cigarette smoking has increased by eight percent a year and lung cancer is now the most common form of cancer found in men. A study in Bangladesh revealed that deaths of children in Dacca were 270 per 1,000 of those born to women who smoked — double the rate of children of nonsmoking mothers.

> *The loss of food and therefore nutrition to the children could be the difference between life and death in countries where children often do not survive beyond the age of five.*

There is also a likelihood that cigarettes sold in the developing countries have a higher tar and nicotine content than in the West. There, these levels have been reduced as a result of antismoking campaigns and government pressure.

In the early 1980s, in Brazil, lung cancer deaths in the state of São Paulo increased nearly seven times in men aged between 50 and 59. The disease was nearly the country's number one killer by the late 1980s. It is the same pattern throughout the developing world with consumption on the increase and few health warnings given when tobacco is so vital to a country's economy.

However, the tobacco industry seems determined to ignore these statistics. "If there is a market for tobacco anywhere we see nothing morally wrong in satisfying that market," said one representative. Meanwhile, others have campaigned for action to be taken. The World Health Organization has issued recommendations on greater control of tobacco production and marketing. It wants to see a gradual drop in the size of tobacco production, priority given to developing food crops instead of tobacco, prohibition of promotion and sales to children, and the introduction of many more health warnings on cigarette packs as there are already in the West.

4

TOBACCO AND TAXES

The history of tobacco shows that it has always aroused strong feelings. Even today, when many governments around the world work closely with tobacco companies in setting prices and collecting taxes, the governments are attacked for not taking stronger action to curb smoking.

The origins of smoking

When tobacco was first used, it was seen as having special or even healing powers. As long ago as 2000 B.C., Indians in South America discovered tobacco as a wild plant and used the smoke from its leaves in religious ceremonies. The Aztecs and Mayans in Central America would put the dried leaves into the hollow stems of reeds to smoke. Later Brazilians used coarse paper instead and cigarettes were invented.

Arawak Indians took tobacco to the West Indies, while European explorers like Christopher Columbus and Sir Walter Raleigh later brought it back from their travels, claiming that the people who used it gained protection from certain diseases. In 1586, Raleigh carefully brought back tobacco seeds from North America to his estate at Youghal in Ireland. There, he had the seeds planted and cultivated. He knew how to manage the growth of the plant, harvest the leaves, cure them, and then how to use a pipe.

The nicotine drug in tobacco was named after Jean Nicot, French ambassador to Portugal, who sent back tobacco seeds to the French court at the end of the sixteenth century. He believed that tobacco smoke was an excellent cure for fever. While tobacco became popular in Europe, it did not arouse real interest in Britain until British soldiers fighting in the Crimean

This carved stone relief shows a god of the Maya of Central America. The god is illustrated smoking a pipe, which has been done by Central American Indians for thousands of years.

War at the start of the nineteenth century were said to have seen enemy soldiers rolling tobacco into strips. They brought the habit back to England.

> *Czar Michael of Russia actually executed those people who had been caught smoking more than once.*

Some people saw the spread of tobacco production and smoking as wrong and sought to discourage it. In 1603, King James I of England wrote a famous essay called *A Counter-Blaste to Tobacco,* in which he called the habit "loathsome to the eye, harmful to the brain, dangerous to the lungs." Czar Michael of Russia actually executed those people who had been caught smoking more than once.

An easy profit

Eventually rulers realized that they could profit from tobacco rather than trying to stamp it out. So they imposed heavy taxes on it. This stopped European farmers from producing tobacco,

TOBACCO

In the nineteenth century high-speed machinery was developed to mass-produce cigarettes, as in this French factory of the 1890s.

and led to the importing of tobacco which was then manufactured into cigarettes. This led in turn to taxes being imposed on cigarette production. The development of high-speed machinery at the end of the nineteenth century led to the mass production of cigarettes, and governments encouraged this because of the extra money it would bring them in taxes.

The economics of tobacco provides $14 billion of all federal tax revenue, and $7 billion of total state and local tax revenues, which is an enormous financial burden off the government. On the other hand, smoking costs the economy $65 billion a year in health care and lost productivity. Every year, tobacco companies try to persuade, or lobby, elected officials to keep any tax increases on tobacco as low as possible. At the same time, health campaigners try to get the same officials to raise taxes, because they see this as a way to discourage smoking.

It is now generally accepted that it is the price of tobacco that has the single biggest influence on how many people smoke and how much tobacco is consumed. It is estimated that for every one percent increase in the real price of a pack of cigarettes there is a corresponding 0.5 percent drop in the amount people smoke. In other words, there is a direct link between price and smoking. "Smokers want to stop and we

know a significant price increase is the trigger that many need
to help them," says Dr. John Dawson, head of the British
Medical Association's scientific division.

Serious concern?

In the U.S., the tobacco industry has enormous power through
politicians from the southern states who represent areas that
have thousands of tobacco farmers. If any law is proposed that
is harmful to tobacco interests it is strongly opposed, even if it
is introduced on health grounds. In the 1970s, President Jimmy
Carter's Secretary for Health, Joe Califano, launched a big
antismoking drive. He set up a special Office on Smoking and
Health to educate the public. This infuriated the tobacco
industry and some of the representatives drove around with
bumper stickers saying "Califano Is Dangerous to My Health."
Califano drew so much opposition from other supporters of
President Carter and the farmers that eventually, in 1979, he
was forced to resign. Califano's critics were worried that the
critical southern states would stop supporting Carter if he
backed such an antitobacco stance.

> It is now generally accepted that it is the price of tobacco that
> has the single biggest influence on how many people smoke
> and how much tobacco is consumed.

Critics of the tobacco industry use Califano's resignation as
an example that the government, in a country where tobacco is
so powerful, is not really able to back an antismoking
campaign. Tobacco industry critics feel governments will stay
loyal to tobacco because of tax revenues and the jobs created
by the industry no matter what the consequences are to public
health. Since 1964, when the Surgeon General first published
its report on the hazards of smoking, the industry has
attempted to reassure its customers by developing low-tar
cigarettes and by widely advertising cigarettes to create the
image that smoking is socially desirable. The Surgeon General
has asserted "there is no such thing as a safe cigarette" and the
reduction in risk of lung cancer from low-tar cigarettes is
"minimal and limited." Some critics feel that governments are
as dependent on cigarette taxes and employment as smokers

are dependent on the costly cigarette habit.

Some governments feel responsible to protect the health of their people. While federal, state, and local governments profit from taxes from the industry and from the purchases made by consumers, governments can also destroy the image of cigarettes as being socially acceptable by restricting cigarette advertising and promotion. Restrictions signify that cigarettes are not socially acceptable.

In the developing countries, the companies also work closely with governments to fix prices and regulate production. "Governmental involvement need not be direct: the official concerned can quietly indicate to the companies that he requires a particular policy to be implemented. No laws are needed and the companies seldom fail to come to heel . . . "

> "The world's seven largest tobacco firms not only control most of the world's tobacco industry, their detailed knowledge puts them in a position of considerable power over national governments . . . officials in developing countries too often serve as mouthpieces for a tobacco firm."

Tax revenue and foreign exchange earnings from tobacco produce so much money for governments that they do not want to upset the relationship with producers. "The world's seven largest tobacco firms not only control most of the world's tobacco industry, their detailed knowledge puts them in a position of considerable power over national governments . . . officials in developing countries too often serve as mouthpieces for a tobacco firm: they are simply being hoodwinked without knowing it," said one critic.

Employment

There is another reason why governments are reluctant to restrict the sale of tobacco — there are millions of jobs provided by the industry.

Workers process the tobacco leaf when it arrives from the warehouse. Once it is blended and dried, it is shredded, fed into rolling machines, and finally portioned out into individual

In a modern cigarette factory, sophisticated machinery can process 5,000 cigarettes a minute.

cigarettes. They are put into packs and then into cartons to be sent to the stores, or for export. Modern machines can make up to 5,000 cigarettes a minute.

Tobacco provides employment for over two million people in the U.S.; 50,000 in Britain, of which 16,500 work in cigarette factories; 42,000 in West Germany; and for 18,000 in both Italy and Spain. The numbers of people employed in Eastern countries are far higher than those in Europe; one factory in Bangkok alone employs 9,000 workers and had an output of 30.5 billion cigarettes in 1980.

5

THE IMAGE MAKERS

The image of smoking promoted by cigarette advertising is clean and cool: a sparkling mountain lake — young people enjoying the outdoors. Then you see a pack of cigarettes. The implication is clear — you too can be one of the beautiful people if you smoke that brand.

What is behind the image? What is clean about the hot smoke you inhale? How does your body react? The advertising and promotion of tobacco, together with sponsorship of sports and the arts, are designed to ensure that people who see these kinds of advertisements do not ask these questions or think about tobacco's addictive properties and dangers.

Creating a desirable and exciting image of tobacco has been crucial to the success of sales around the world. It is precisely because of the acknowledged health risks to smokers that the industry has spent literally billions of dollars telling people that one particular brand of cigarette has "come a long way," and inviting people to "come to where the flavor is." It is an attempt to convince people that smoking is not harmful but glamorous, and is associated with attractiveness and romance, power and sporting achievement. To that end, $2 billion every year is spent on tobacco advertising in the U.S. In Britain the figure is around $170 million a year.

A lack of control

In many countries there is a certain amount of restriction on tobacco advertising. However, the picture is different in the developing world. Advertising images are used there that would never be allowed in the U.S. or Europe. One in Nigeria shows a university graduate seated at his desk in his academic gown

Tobacco advertising is widespread in developing countries where the fastest-growing markets are to be found.

smoking a Varsity cigarette. "He's a Varsity man. He feels that a Varsity cigarette helps him to concentrate. He likes the way the superfine menthol clears his head," runs the ad.

> *Africa has some countries that cannot supply enough food for their people, yet in tiny villages hit by drought and famine there are posters promoting cigarettes.*

A brand in Africa is called Life and was promoted in a poster declaring that "Life is Great." Africa has some countries that cannot supply enough food for their people, yet in tiny villages hit by drought and famine there are posters promoting a brand of cigarettes that claim it is "The best tobacco money can buy." A study of cigarette marketing in four countries, Ghana, Kenya, Malaysia, and Thailand, said that cigarettes were easily available in all parts of these countries and that posters were everywhere. In Kenya, advertisements present cigarette smoking as a socially desirable custom by showing young, happy, and successful people: "Not much is done to regulate where and when consumers can smoke and there has been little antismoking information," reports the study.

TOBACCO

Images

The images used in cigarette advertising are tailored to the kind of people that the companies believe will buy each particular brand of cigarettes. Sex appeal is the commonest way to entice consumers. Feminine images are sometimes used to promote slim, long cigarettes and menthol brands, such as Eve in the U.S. and Miss Blanche in The Netherlands. However, masculine images are more common and such brands as Marlboro, Winston, and Camel have been the most successful in conveying a "macho" or cowboy image that links smoking to manliness and success.

> *Sex appeal is the commonest way to entice consumers.*

This cigarette advertisement in a Lesotho, South Africa, market shows a healthy outdoor image in association with cigarettes.

Sports are also employed to appeal to the young, with such names as Sportsman in Africa and Jockey Club in Argentina. Images associated with relaxation and the older man are often suggested in pipe tobacco advertising, with cigars and luxury brands like Dunhill.

Class appeal also features in cigarette advertising, promoting the idea that smoking is associated with high social status and spending power. One Taiwanese brand is simply called Wealth. In terms of nationality, some brands suggest local ties, such as Cleopatra in Egypt, while others have an international image that means they can sell well in the duty-free shops of airports all around the world.

Sponsorship

Sponsorship of sports and the arts by tobacco firms has increased greatly in the last 20 years. The indirect connection with a healthy industry such as sports helps to promote the tobacco image as well. Some critics believe that this is a way of getting around the restrictions on direct advertising.

If television viewers can see billboards with cigarette brand names around sports stadiums and auto-racing circuits, then it is an excellent way of having their product promoted. Billboards advertising cigarettes are seen by millions of fans, particularly impressionable young people. Sponsorship is formulated to change the public's negative conception of cigarettes and cigarette companies. Sponsorship of the arts helps the tobacco industry enhance an image of respectability and prestige.

> *The indirect connection with a healthy industry such as sports helps to promote the tobacco image as well.*

Marlboro's move into Formula One auto-racing was accompanied by publicity stating that "we are the number one brand in the world. What we wanted was to promote a particular image of adventure, of courage, or virility." Car-racing is seen as a glamorous, exciting sport enjoyed by bold, daring individuals, and gets multinational coverage; it is the most sponsored of all sports by tobacco companies.

TOBACCO

In May 1990, Ayrton Senna of Brazil shattered the Formula 1 speed record, giving Marlboro, the sponsor, additional advertising.

A disturbing new trend is growing, ironically among athletes and young people — an increase in the use of smokeless tobacco. Snuff, chewing tobacco, and "cigarettes" that are not lit but only "puffed" are increasing in sales. The newest consumers are teenagers and younger children. Many users are unaware that smokeless tobacco is harmful. It can cause addiction, mouth disease, and oral cancer. The great baseball player, Babe Ruth, a tobacco chewer, died of oral cancer. To appeal to the young, popular athletes and celebrities are paid by the tobacco companies to promote these products.

Counterimages

In a film made for television called *Death in the West*, the rugged image of the Marlboro cowboy was directly challenged. The filmmakers went out West and interviewed six real-life cowboys, exactly the same sort as in the advertisements. However, these were different because they were all heavy smokers who were seriously ill from cancer or emphysema. All but one of those interviewed died soon after the program was shown.

> "I thought that to be a man you had to have a cigarette in your mouth. It took me years to discover that all I got out of it was lung cancer."

"I started smoking when I was a kid following these bronco busters. I thought that to be a man you had to have a cigarette in your mouth. It took me years to discover that all I got out of it was lung cancer," said one cowboy. The film shows a tobacco executive for Philip Morris, which produces Marlboro, saying, "I think that if the company as a whole believed cigarettes were really harmful, we would not be in the business. We're a very moralistic company." It is significant that this same company obtained an injunction that prevents *Death in the West* from being broadcast again.

SMOKING AND ADDICTION

Smoking-related diseases cause 350,000 deaths in the U.S. each year, 17.2 percent of all deaths in this country annually. Cigarette smoking is the single most preventable cause of death in our society. A 25-year-old man who smokes a pack of cigarettes a day, reduces his lifespan by about 4.5 years; each cigarette chops off five minutes from his life. Cigarettes cause more premature deaths than AIDS, cocaine, heroin, alcohol, fire, automobile accidents, homicide, and suicide combined.

> *"Most people know it causes lung cancer and that it's bad for your heart, but you always think you're going to be the exception."*

Tobacco is, quite literally, a killer. Although there has been a consistent drop in people smoking in the last ten years, 40 percent of heavy smokers die before the age of 65 compared with 15 percent of nonsmokers. One smoker who had up to 15 cigarettes a day for three years said, "Most people know it causes lung cancer and that it's bad for your heart, but you always think you're going to be the exception." Another 30-a-day smoker confessed that his family's experiences were making him think twice about the habit: "I've already lost two aunts from emphysema. And my father is very sick. He can't breathe properly. He just sits there gasping."

> *" . . . my father is very sick. He can't breathe properly. He just sits there gasping."*

Why smoking is dangerous

Research has shown that tobacco smoke contains several poisonous substances that can be damaging to the body. It also contains hundreds of other compounds. Some of these are:

Nicotine	an oily chemical that acts as a powerful drug
Ammonia	a chemical used in household cleaning powders and in explosives
Butane	the gas used in lighters and in some camping stoves
Carbon monoxide	a very poisonous gas also found in the exhaust fumes of cars

These four compounds can be deadly. If the amount of nicotine contained in a small cigar, for example, was injected directly into a person, he or she would die within a minute. Smoked in a cigarette, the nicotine is less powerful and the body is able to adjust to its poisons over a period of time.

In the act of smoking a filter cigarette, most of these compounds are joined together into a dark, sticky substance known as tobacco tar, which can cause cancer in living tissue. The more you smoke of a cigarette the less the tar is diluted, so that the last third gives the most nicotine and tar. After inhaling a cigarette, the body keeps all the carbon monoxide, over 90 percent of the nicotine, and 70 percent of the tar given off.

> *If the amount of nicotine contained in a small cigar, for example, was injected directly into a person, he or she would die within a minute.*

The body needs oxygen to breathe, and a substance in the blood called hemoglobin carries the oxygen from the lungs into the bloodstream. When you smoke, the hemoglobin latches onto the carbon monoxide instead, so less oxygen is released through the body. Heavy smokers can have the oxygen-carrying power of their blood cut by as much as 15 percent. This explains why smokers often get short of breath

TOBACCO

Nicotine in tobacco reaches the brain in less than 30 seconds. It depresses the brain and nervous system, making the smoker feel relaxed.

Traffic pollutes the air with carbon monoxide. This very poisonous gas is also breathed into the lungs every time a cigarette is smoked.

when they try to exert energy such as when running for a bus or even just climbing the stairs.

The nicotine in the tar makes the heart beat faster than it should and tends to raise blood pressure. It has an effect on the brain and nervous system by giving a feeling of being calmer and even relaxed. This happens very quickly. The nicotine reaches the brain in less than 30 seconds after inhaling. It is so effective the smoker wants more and more . . . Soon, he or she is smoking regularly and is hooked. It is only recently that the smoking habit has been officially described as addictive; in other words it has been recognized that it is a drug.

Addiction

A report was produced in 1988 by the Surgeon General, the chief American medical officer for health. It was called *The Health Consequences of Smoking: Nicotine Addiction*. After examining all the evidence, it came to three conclusions:

1. Cigarettes and other forms of tobacco are addictive.
2. Nicotine is the drug in tobacco that causes addiction.
3. The medical and behavioral processes that determine tobacco addiction are similar to those that determine addiction to drugs such as heroin and cocaine.

After inhaling a cigarette, the body keeps all the carbon monoxide, over 90 percent of the nicotine, and 70 percent of the tar given off.

The Surgeon General's influential report, the result of much research, said that with regular use, levels of nicotine gathered in the body during the day and lasted overnight. "Thus, daily tobacco users are exposed to the effects of nicotine for 24 hours each day." The report also said that smokers performed better on tasks requiring concentration, but that smoking did not improve general learning. Stress appeared to increase the amount people smoked and in general smokers weighed less than nonsmokers, about eight pounds less on average. A good many smokers who stop smoking gain weight, but this is often only a temporary situation. In any case, smoking is not a good form of weight control.

TOBACCO

The filter on the end of this cigarette is stained yellow by tobacco tar, which can cause cancer.

Overall, the Surgeon General's report was a crucial addition to the tobacco debate because it placed tobacco firmly in its place with other drugs that damage people who become dependent on them. The report advised that "Tobacco use is a disorder that can be remedied through medical attention. Therefore, it should be approached by health care providers just as other substance-use disorders are approached, with knowledge, understanding, and persistence."

> " . . . daily tobacco users are exposed to the effects of nicotine for 24 hours each day."

In 1983, the Royal College of Physicians in London, England, produced a report called *Health or Smoking.* This was one of several reports that really sounded the alarm about the health hazards of tobacco. It stated, "While smoking behavior clearly demonstrates all the features of a habit, there is little doubt too that the smokers derive pleasure from smoking and persist with the habit in order to satisfy their need for these pleasurable sensations. They thus become dependent on or addicted to smoking." Smokers are doubly hooked: to the nicotine in the smoke and to the rituals, like lighting up and puffing, that surround smoking.

Smokers feel sick if they stop smoking, and their withdrawal symptoms can be stopped by more nicotine. There is evidence that when the level of nicotine goes down in cigarettes, people smoke more to compensate. Between 1969 and 1973, the average nicotine content of cigarettes fell by 32 percent. In the same period the annual number of cigarettes consumed per smoker rose, by about 18 percent in both men and women.

7

KILLER TOBACCO

In 1989, scientists proved that there is a link between smoking and cancer. A report published in the journal *Nature* revealed that when cigarettes are smoked, the chemicals involved damage the DNA at the heart of each human cell, which controls our normal growth patterns. The report found that when people had given up smoking for five years, they registered only low levels of DNA damage similar to that of nonsmokers.

> *Smoking is the direct cause of lung cancer. It also increases the risk of cancer of the mouth, throat, esophagus, bladder, and probably the pancreas.*

Despite this increased knowledge about the risks of tobacco, people still continue to smoke, and many develop diseases. Smoking is a direct cause of lung cancer. It also increases the risk of cancer of the mouth, throat, esophagus, bladder, and probably the pancreas. There is also some evidence that in women smoking may be a cause of cancer of the cervix.

Lung cancer

In 1986, cigarettes were found to be the direct cause of 141,600 out of the 472,000 deaths from cancer in the U.S. Lung cancer kills more people than any other type of cancer. In 1985, 40,860 people in the U.K. died from it.

Although lung cancer has been declining slightly in men under 65 in the last 20 years, it is still rising among women. In

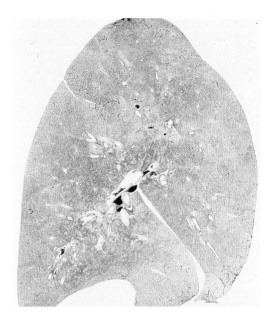

This section of a healthy human lung is pink and mainly clear of any irritants.

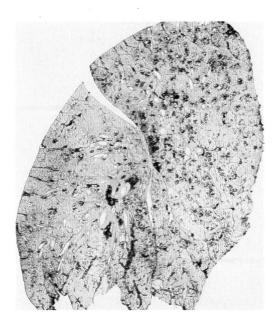

This section of a human lung from a smoker is discolored and full of tar deposits from cigarettes.

the U.S., lung cancer has overtaken breast cancer as the leading cancer killer among women. The risk of lung cancer increases directly with the number of cigarettes smoked.

The annual death rate from lung cancer of male nonsmokers per 100,000 is 10. However, for the person smoking up to 14 cigarettes a day it is 78 per 100,000 and for someone smoking 25 or more it is 251 per 100,000. When smokers give up smoking, the risk of developing lung cancer stops increasing as they get older. After 10 or 15 years, an ex-smoker's risk is only slightly more than that of someone who has never smoked.

Between 1954 and 1971, a study of doctors who smoked was made. It showed that in that period the proportion of male doctors who smoked fell by half. The death rate from lung cancer among male doctors fell by 25 percent, while it jumped up by 25 percent in the population as a whole.

Coronary heart disease

Every year, hundreds of thousands of people die from heart attacks, and in the West at least half of these are caused by smoking. The nicotine in tobacco makes the heart work harder while the carbon monoxide reduces the vital supply of oxygen that the heart needs. This can lead to severe chest pains, heart attacks, and death. The smoker is at a two to three times greater risk of having such an attack than is a nonsmoker.

Even more at risk are people who are unhealthy in other

The nicotine in tobacco makes the heart work harder while the carbon monoxide reduces the vital supply of oxygen it needs. This can lead to severe chest pains, heart attacks, and death.

ways as well — for instance, those who have a high level of cholesterol in their blood from eating too many fatty foods. Stopping smoking after a heart attack could lead to as many as 10,000 fewer deaths each year, of both men and women.

Chronic bronchitis and emphysema

When smokers cough it is probably an early sign of bronchitis. This comes about because the lungs and air passages are not

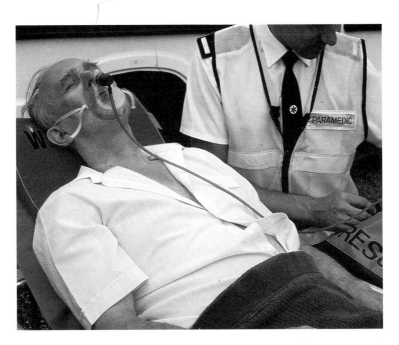

Heart attacks can be caused by smoking, which reduces the oxygen supply, raises the blood pressure, and makes the heart work harder.

able to get rid of the mucus and phlegm that gather normally in everybody's systems. The tobacco smoke weakens the body's ability to rid itself of this, and the person has to cough to force the matter out of their system. Eventually, the lungs become infected and the sufferer finds it very difficult to breathe properly.

Emphysema is a similar disease of the lungs which produces breathlessness. Parts of the walls of the air sacs throughout the lungs are destroyed, which makes it more difficult for the blood to take up oxygen. The smoker literally gasps for breath.

> *"Buerger's Disease only happens to smokers. So far it's meant the amputation of both his legs. Unless he stops smoking he'll lose his hands and arms. Yet still he smokes."*

Chronic bronchitis and emphysema are very rare in nonsmokers. A recent research project interviewed two men who had ruined their lives by constant smoking. "Joe David is

73. A lifetime's smoking has given him bronchitis, two heart attacks, and emphysema. Now he's so short of breath he can barely brush his teeth, let alone hold a decent conversation." Edward Oliver has what is known as Buerger's Disease: "Buerger's Disease only happens to smokers. So far it's meant the amputation of both his legs. Unless he stops smoking he'll lose his hands and arms. Yet still he smokes."

Passive smoking

Some people argue that smoking is very much an individual habit, and that people should be able to do as they please because no one else is harmed. These people believe that it is an issue of individual freedom. However, there is growing evidence that nonsmokers are harmed by smoking. This arises from what is called passive smoking, or environmental tobacco smoke (ets).

Surveys have recently been done proving that passive smoking, absorbing smoke from someone else's cigarette, is harmful. Children with smoking parents can "smoke" 80 cigarettes a year.

The nonsmoker can breathe in both sidestream smoke from a cigarette lying on an ashtray and mainstream smoke that is breathed out by the smoker. This is obviously worse for people in confined spaces. If they work in offices, socialize in clubs, or live with a smoker at home, they are at risk.

Smoke causes annoyance to many nonsmokers by making hair and clothes smell unpleasant. More seriously, smoke can cause symptoms such as eye irritation, headaches, coughs, sore throats, dizziness, and nausea. People with asthma or bronchitis will suffer from many of the symptoms more acutely.

> . . . smoke can cause symptoms such as eye irritation, headaches, coughs, sore throats, dizziness, and nausea.

In 1988, a British government-sponsored report looked at the long-term dangers for the passive smoker. "The findings overall are consistent with there being a small increase in the risk of lung cancer from exposure to passive smoking in the range of 10 to 30 percent." This means that there might be one to three extra lung cancer deaths a year per 100,000 nonsmokers who are regularly exposed to passive smoke. Protecting nonsmokers from passive smoke is one of the most powerful reasons behind the push in the United States for bans on smoking in many offices, special nonsmoking areas in most restaurants, and smoking bans on all forms of public transportation.

8

THE YOUNG ONES

In order for cigarette companies to maintain their sales, they must recruit 2,190,000 new smokers each year. Cigarette advertising is aimed at the young. For example, the romance and adventure of Marlboro Country has a strong appeal to both young male and female consumers. It is the most widely sold packaged product in the world, and the most popular beginner cigarette. More Marlboros are sold than Coca-Cola. The tobacco industry is accused of "selling death," and with sales of $30 billion dollars a year it will continue to seek the uninitiated.

> *"One survey found that one percent had tried a cigarette before the age of five."*

Why young people smoke

Dr. Anne Charlton, who investigates for the Cancer Research Campaign, says that many people start to smoke at an early age. "One survey found that one percent had tried a cigarette before the age of five. With the under-11's it's mostly for appearance. Boys tend to start earlier, although young girls think smoking makes them look sophisticated. After 11 and 12 there is a big change. They seem to feel that cigarettes give them something positive. They have the idea that a cigarette calms their nerves, gives them confidence — this is particularly true of girls. Boys are more likely to smoke with their friends to be part of a crowd."

There are many reasons why young people smoke. Many enjoy the ritual of opening the pack and offering cigarettes.

Some children start smoking at a very early age. This boy is only 10 years old.

Some smoke as a reaction to stress; smoking is often seen as one answer to unemployment and boredom. Frequently smoking is used to help boost confidence at a party or club, or when meeting strangers.

Dr. Charlton also thinks that the images young people see on television and in tobacco advertising play a big part. "I was watching the film *Ghostbusters* recently and one of the main characters seemed to light up a cigarette every time a ghost appeared. Yet this is a film aimed at young people."

Studies have shown that the smoking habits of parents are crucial, as is whether they approve or disapprove of the habit. Any child, smoker or not, is 1.5 times more likely to be away from school if his or her parents smoke. The risk increases if the smoker is the mother.

A danger to health

Schoolchildren who smoke regularly are more likely to be absent from school than nonsmokers. They may be absent because of minor ailments such as colds, flu, tonsilitis, and stomach disorders. Children who smoke are more liable to get coughs and increased phlegm, and are more likely to have

Children whose mothers have smoked during pregnancy are often born smaller than those of nonsmoking parents. They also have more respiratory infections.

respiratory diseases than nonsmokers. A youngster who smokes is probably a reflection of parents who smoke.

The earlier children become regular smokers and continue with the habit as adults, the greater the risk of dying prematurely. Children are also more prone to the risk of passive smoking. A study of children who lived in houses where both parents smoked showed that the children were receiving an amount of nicotine equivalent to 80 cigarettes a year. Bronchitis and other respiratory diseases are much more common in the first year of life in children who have one or more smoking parents.

In young women smoking brings the added threat of cancer of the cervix. Research done in 1988 showed they are twice as likely to develop the disease. Smoking damages the defense cells that protect against disease. Albert Singer, a medical expert who sees many women with cervical cancer, says that the youngest woman he had found to show the early stages of the disease was 14 years old and a heavy smoker. He says, "This cannot go on. It seems to be an epidemic. We are extremely worried about the numbers of young women who smoke." Also, smoking by women who take oral contraception heightens their risk of cardiovascular disease.

Attracting the young

Despite restrictions imposed by governments, the tobacco companies know that the teenage and youth market is a profitable one which they must appeal to. According to market research carried out for one company: "For the young smoker, the cigarette is not yet an integral part of life . . . . In the young smoker's mind a cigarette falls into the same category as wine, beer, shaving, wearing a bra (or purposely not wearing one), declaration of independence, and striving for self identity . . . a cigarette is associated with introduction to sex life, with courtship, with smoking 'pot,' and keeping late studying hours."

The advice in this report was that in order to attract young people starting to smoke, cigarettes should be presented as an initiation into the adult world. It also stressed that reference to health and "health-related points" should be avoided.

The Surgeon General realized the danger to the young of such exposure. "To maintain momentum toward a smoke-free

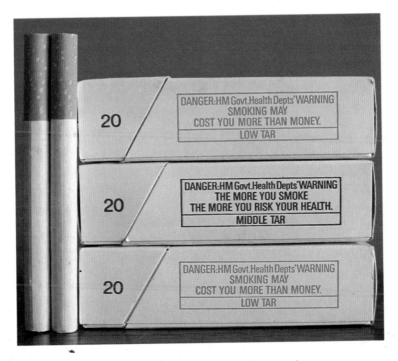

Warnings about the danger of smoking have been written on cigarette packs and advertisements in several countries.

TOBACCO

In China, there are 200 million smokers of all ages. In order to encourage a smoke-free society it is important to educate the young about the risks to health of smoking.

society, we must take steps to prevent young people from beginning to smoke. First, we must ensure that every child in every school in this country is educated as to health risks and the addictive nature of tobacco use. Second, warning labels regarding the addictive nature of tobacco use should be required for all tobacco packages and advertisements. Young people in particular may not be aware of the risk of tobacco addiction. Finally, parents and other role models should discourage smoking and other forms of tobacco use among young people. Parents who quit set an example for their children."

The news about young people and smoking is not all bad. According to a recent National Institute on Drug Abuse study, during the time between 1975 and 1985, the number of all graduating high school senior males who smoked daily dropped from 27 percent to 18 percent. Surveys of high school senior females shows a decline in smoking from 26 percent in 1976 to 21 percent in 1985.

STUBBING OUT SMOKING

"After almost choking to death through early morning coughing, I put cigarettes, tobacco, three good pipes, and a lighter, all in the furnace at work and vowed I would never smoke again. That was eight year ago." This smoker who had smoked 20 cigarettes a day for 20 years is the living proof that it is possible to give up.

> *"After almost choking to death through early morning coughing, I put cigarettes, tobacco, three good pipes, and a lighter, all in the furnace at work and vowed I would never smoke again. That was eight years ago."*

People often would like to quit smoking but they usually need some trigger such as seeing someone suffering from the effects of tobacco to make the final decision. The issue of whether to continue smoking or stop also involves a question — how much control do we have over our own health and our own bodies?

The decision to give up smoking is like deciding to lose weight because we cannot fit into certain clothes. We want to feel more comfortable about ourselves and be more attractive to others. This ties in with the fact that people tend to be more health-conscious than they used to be. The advantages of high-fiber foods and disadvantages of eating foods containing lots of fat and sugar are more widely known. More people are exercising and keeping fit.

On the other hand, people cannot be forced to change their habits overnight. If they were, it might have the opposite effect.

TOBACCO

People in developed countries have become much more health conscious in recent years. They exercise more, eat better, and are smoking less.

Health education in schools and from health professionals such as doctors and specialists is the way to show those who might be attracted to tobacco that, in the end, it is just not worth it.

Cutting down the death and sickness toll from tobacco takes place on two levels: first, at the individual, personal level, and second, on the broader international, governmental, and institutional level. The two levels are obviously linked because government policy or action by employers can influence individuals. Sometimes the statistics speak for themselves. Every year since 1964, an average 1.5 million Americans quit smoking. However, 50 million Americans still continue the habit. In 1990, 18.9 million Americans (37.8 percent of all smokers) participated in The Great American Smokeout, which is an annual event held the Thursday before Thanksgiving by the American Cancer Society. Smokers are urged to give up or cut back on their tobacco use. The American Cancer Society provides millions of adults and children with education on the hazards of smoking, and prevention and cessation programs. The American Cancer Society and the American Lung Association have information and programs directed toward teenagers.

Individual action

Some people get very angry about smoking because they argue that it interferes with their freedom to breathe unpolluted air or, at least, air not filled with tobacco smoke. Occasionally they take the law into their own hands. In New York, it was reported that commuters beat up a smoker at a train station. An English newspaper reported: "A youth in a no-smoking train compartment who sneeringly blew smoke at a middle-aged woman who politely asked him to stub his cigarette got his comeuppance. She set off a fire extinguisher and drenched him." This sort of extreme behavior is not typical, but activism has mobilized public opinion against smoking in public places.

Others have decided that the law can be turned to advantage in the battle with the tobacco companies. In 1988, legal history was made in the U.S. when a jury awarded damages of $400,000 to Tony Cipollone of New Jersey, whose wife died at the age of 53 from lung cancer. (The decision was overturned on appeal.) She smoked 60 cigarettes a day for 40 years, and the companies who manufactured the brands she smoked were held to be partly responsible for her death.

There have been a number of antismoking campaigns, such as "The Great American Smokeout," which encourage people to give up smoking.

TOBACCO

Lawyers for Mr. Cipollone produced hundreds of confidential documents to show that companies knew as early as the 1950s that there was a link between smoking and cancer. Yet they carried advertisements saying that brands were "just what the doctor ordered." After the case, tobacco shares only fell marginally on Wall Street and the London Stock Exchange, showing just how powerful the tobacco companies are.

> In 1988, legal history was made in the U.S. when a jury awarded damages of $400,000 to a man whose wife died from lung cancer.

The Cipollone case cost over $1.5 million to fight . It is the financial burden that is one of the biggest barriers to going to court. However, in 1988, a man in Northern Ireland was awarded legal aid to pursue his case. John Dean, an unemployed man from Newtownards, is suing a tobacco company for a condition that severely limits his ability to walk. His attorneys have prepared a claim that the company was negligent in not warning him of the dangers of smoking. When he started smoking, there were no health warnings on cigarette packs, just as in the case of Mrs. Cipollone.

> "I stopped for an hour, then two, then three hours, and so on. I bragged to my friends that I had stopped. Then I didn't dare lose face. Instead, I nibbled carrots nonstop."

Quitting

The evidence that exists suggests that many smokers would like to give up the habit if they could, and it can be done. One successful person said: "I stopped for an hour, then two, then three hours, and so on. I bragged to my friends that I had stopped. Then I didn't dare lose face. Instead, I nibbled carrots nonstop." One of the largest surveys of smokers' attitudes was carried out by a company who interviewed 1,300 smokers and 2,700 nonsmokers. Of these, 70 percent of all smokers had tried to give up, and a half of these had made at least three attempts.

The three main reasons for giving up were expense, illness, and social pressure. In the survey, 30 percent said they found themselves "smoking without really enjoying it" fairly often. No more than 37 percent could think of going a day without a cigarette, and only 13 percent could survive a week. Smokers consumed an average of 18.5 cigarettes a day, although many had switched to lower tar brands.

> *"I tried three times. Finally, I kept a pack on me so I had to face up to it. I used willpower and nearly went mad for three weeks."*

Overall, 40 percent of the sample favored a total ban on smoking in public places. Smokers say kicking the habit is tough but it can be done. "I tried three times. Finally, I kept a pack on me so I had to face up to it. I used willpower and nearly went mad for three weeks," said one ex-smoker who had smoked 30 cigarettes a day for six years.

Feeling good

People invent all kinds of arguments to put off making decisions on smoking. These include, "I'll lose my only pleasure in life" or "I can't inflict it on my family — I'd be impossible to live with." To excuses like this, health education groups reply that life is much more worthwhile living as a nonsmoker. For instance, nonsmokers are able to taste and enjoy their food much more. Smokers are already inflicting suffering on their families by polluting the atmosphere.

The American Heart Association (AHA) issues guidelines for quitting which include four points:

1. List all the reasons why you want to quit and, every night before bed, repeat one of the reasons ten times.
2. Decide positively you want to quit.
3. Develop strong personal reasons such as the time wasted smoking cigarettes, etc.
4. Set a target date such as your birthday for quitting and stick to it.

The AHA points out as encouragement that quitting will bring immediate positive results. "Within 12 hours after you have your last cigarette, your body will begin to heal itself. The levels of carbon monoxide and nicotine in your system will decline rapidly and your heart and lungs will begin to repair some of the damage caused by cigarette smoke.

> *"Within 12 hours after you have your last cigarette, your body will begin to heal itself. The levels of carbon monoxide and nicotine in your system will decline rapidly and your heart and lungs will begin to repair some of the damage caused by cigarette smoke."*

"Within a few days, you will begin to notice some remarkable changes in your body. Your sense of smell and taste will return. Your smoker's hack will disappear. Your digestive system will return to normal. Most important of all, you will feel really alive — clear-headed, full of energy and strength. You will be breathing easier. You will be able to climb a hill or a flight of stairs without becoming winded or dizzy. And you will be free from the mess, smell, inconvenience, expense, and dependence of cigarette smoking."

Collective action

The World Health Organization (WHO) has spoken out strongly against tobacco as a health hazard. It has even set up a top-level unit especially to work against the effects of the tobacco industry. WHO's Regional Committee for Europe held a conference on tobacco in Madrid in 1988 and people from 30 countries attended to discuss health and education issues.

Many governments and states are now moving toward greater restrictions or outright bans on smoking, often as a reaction to growing complaints about passive smoking. In both California and New York, all public buildings are now smoke-free zones, and San Francisco has banned smoking on its public transportation.

The Australian government has banned smoking on all flights by Australian international airlines, adding to the 15 year old ban on smoking on public transportation and in cinemas. Smoking is not permitted in government offices and in schools in Australia.

Canada has ended tobacco advertising and frozen spending by industry on sponsorship. It has guaranteed all state employees the right to a smoke-free workplace and ensured smoke-free provision on all public transportation. These laws were passed after two years' of campaigning by health groups.

In The Netherlands, a new tougher advertising code has been introduced. Advertisements cannot link smoking with sports and people under 25 are not allowed to appear in advertisements promoting smoking. Smoking in all public places has now been banned in the Greek region of Cyprus. In restaurants, bars, and cafés it is permitted, provided the owner posts health warnings.

Jordan is also banning smoking in public places, while the Sudan has done the same and also banned tobacco advertising. In Belgium, Spain, and Norway smoking in most public buildings is prohibited. In Britain smoking is banned on the London underground system and on all British Airways domestic flights. The U.S. Congress has passed a law that forbids smoking on all flights of less than six hours.

Companies are now much more willing to provide a safer and healthier environment for their workforce. They see it as

A major fire at a subway station in London, England, in 1987 killed over 30 people. The fire appeared to have been started by a discarded cigarette — a common cause of fires.

in their self-interest to keep health-care costs down and to prevent absenteeism and improve working conditions. The oil giant BP has banned smoking from all shared offices, corridors, meeting-rooms, and restrooms, while many other large companies have introduced similar no-smoking policies.

Environmental health officers who work for local authorities are being stricter in enforcing health and safety at work. One officer said, "If an employer fails to do anything following complaints, then we will consider taking legal action."

The Surgeon General has called for a "smoke-free society by the year 2000." With the tremendous influence of the tobacco companies, this will be a difficult goal to achieve, but not impossible. The federal government could establish a strong antismoking campaign to educate the public, especially young people, about the dangers of tobacco. With the help of the Department of Agriculture, tobacco farmers could learn how to grow and market other crops, such as fruits and vegetables. Personal injury lawsuits by smokers and passive smokers, litigation by state and federal governments (which pay billions of dollars to smoking-related health care costs) to recover costs, and legal action taken by individuals due to fires caused by cigarettes could reduce the power of the tobacco industry.

Tobacco companies themselves can help cut the annual death toll from their products by enforcing the ban on sales to children. They could also agree to tougher warnings on their products and stop all sponsorship that links smoking with pleasurable or sporting activities.

In the long term, the tobacco companies could consider transferring their enormous resources into producing other products and services that people need but which do not kill them or others. That would require major policy decisions, perhaps at the level of governments. The governments themselves would have to decide that the health arguments on smoking were more powerful than the revenue that is gained from taxes on tobacco products. Such decisions would mean that the politicians in power would have to take a truly firm stand against the powerful tobacco industry.

INFORMATION

United States
American Cancer Society
1599 Clifton Road NE
Atlanta, GA 30329

American Heart Association
7320 Greenville Avenue
Dallas, TX 75231

American Lung Association
1740 Broadway
New York, NY 10019

Center for Science in the Public Interest
1501 16th Street NW
Washington DC 20036

Office of the Secretary
Department of Education
400 Maryland Avenue SW, Room 4181
Washington DC 20202

Canada
Addiction Research Foundation
33 Russell Street
Toronto, Ontario M5S 2S1

Canadian Cancer Society
10 Alcorn Avenue
Toronto, Ontario M4V 3B1

Canadian Heart Foundation
American Heart Association, Suite 1200
1 Nicholas Street
Ottawa, Ontario K1N7-B7

The Canadian Lung Association
75 Albert Street, Suite 908
Ottawa, Ontario K1P 5E7

INDEX

Library of Congress Cataloging-in-Publication Data

Cohen, Philip.
    Tobacco / written by Philip Cohen.
       p. cm. — (Drugs — the complete story)
    Includes index.
    Summary: Examines the role of tobacco as a major economic, political, social, and health issue. Includes information on the tobacco industry and on the hazards of smoking.
    ISBN 0-8114-3202-5   —   ISBN 0-8114-3207-6 (soft cover)
    1. Tobacco habit — Juvenile literature.   2. Smoking — Juvenile literature.   3. Tobacco — Physiological effect — Juvenile literature.   4. Tobacco industry — Juvenile literature.   [1. Tobacco habit. 2. Smoking. 3. Tobacco — Physiological effect. 4. Tobacco industry.] I. Title. II. Series.
    HV5733.C58   1992
    362.29'6 — dc20
                                     91-32583
                                       CIP AC

Consultants: Kenneth J. Schmidt, Passaic County, N.J., Probation Dept.; Marilyn Devroye, consultant for Psychiatric Institutes of America, Washington, DC.

Editors: Margaret Sinclair, Gina Kulch

Cover design by Joyce Spicer

Typeset by Tom Fenton Studio, Neptune, NJ
Printed and bound by Lake Book, Melrose Park, IL

Photographic Credits
Cover: © James Minor, *inset:* © Larry Lefever/Grant Heilman, Inc. page 6 Europe Against Cancer; 2, 7 D; Charlwood/Tropix Photo Library; 11 Sarah Errington/Hutchinson Library; 12 S, Bohling; 14 M Jory/Tropix; 17 Alan Hutchinson Library; 19a & b J. Allan Cash; 3, 20 Robert Aberman/Hutchinson Library; 25 Nick Saunders/Barbara Heller Photo Library; 26 Ann Ronan Picture Library; 3, 29 Topham Picture Source; 31 D. Charlwood/Tropix Photo Library; 32 Liba Taylor/Hutchinson Library; 34 Associate Press/Topham; 38a Hutchison Library, 38b J. G. Fuller/Hutchinson Library; 40 M. Jory/Tropix Photo Library; 43a & b James Stevenson/Science Photo Library; 45 Adam Hart-Davis/Science Photo Library; 46 David Hoffman; 49 J. Allan Cash; 50 Janine Wiedel; 51 J. Allan Cash; 52 Michael Macintyre/Hutchingson Library; 54 Brian Gibbs/Topham, 55, 59 Associated Press/Topham.

Original text and illustrations
© Heinemann Educational Books Ltd.. 1991

64